"Abraham Smith is one of my favorite living poets keeping the art form alive. He stokes the fires of imagination and his persistence keeps the cinders of inspiration smoldering. It is a joy to read his work and a thrill to hear him read it in person."

- Margo Price

"The mists that hover over a meadow first thing in the morning do not disappear; rather they sublime into the day or, as Thoreau once put it, they "conform to the fashions of eternity." In One Warm Morning, Abraham Smith likewise hovers gently over his words as they sublime, effortlessly it seems, into an eternity of free access and inviolable intimacy. Along the way, the music they make is the most companionable that I know."

- Donald Revell

"Abraham Smith takes a long walk on a warm morning and we are lucky to be invited along as he shows us the mind is not a fact but a motion. And a music! of "hummingbirds / historical jazzes / corks in rapids," and a holy lot more. Smith caroms from one association to the next –a deerfly bite, a bad tattoo, "a cold bleacher / at the last homegame of the year" – as if there were no bounds to consciousness, as if "we must have what's next" and "go on go on go on go on," as if the joy's all in the movement. It is! You'll wish it wouldn't end."

- Joel Brouwer

one warm morning

abraham smith

STUBBORN MULE PRESS
DEVIL'S ELBOW, MO

Stubborn Mule Press
Devil's Elbow, Missouri

Copyright © Abraham Smith, 2024

First Edition: 1 3 5 7 9 10 8 6 4 2

ISBN: 978-1-958182-91-8

LCCN: 2024946151

Author photo: Abraham Smith

Acknowledgments:

The author wishes to thank the Ozarkian Quixote Society and Mark and Tony at the Osage Arts Community. With extra ceiling-confetti shoutouts to Ryberg for his thunder-down-the-mountain poetry and lighthouse-like editorial acumen and care.

Table of Contents:

for ma, the goose, and cma

yet I persist
by explosive equilibria
by unmonitored task
by telepathic combining

- Will Alexander

one warm morning

out walking
one fine morning
and warm and warming

may one
a fine one
may i be one
falls in
natural as
wind is the placer

wooden bleachers
member how they slid
folded up in
clutter shudder clean

first river swim
of the year our
shout share chasin
fair molting
up the well knot

cowshit cold rock crayfish
crutchsaw their names
pinch for reasons
related to being
banana rearview
flesh light

there was a child
in the 2nd grade
could tell

the lord's prayer
in pig latin
she had a kid brother
they sd never would grow
never has still

they sd
goes ahead
takes the air
from the room

guess it strolls
air for spare
all and all i am
limpin into bozeman
on the gossip of ages

remember how
janitors with little sticks
were they neutered broomsticks
sandwiched the works

a logjam cured
only slicker
and you were sicker
than the lot

felt the feeling
of caught up in
upended eaten
a gushing green
and yellowing spray
and seeping pieces

to tell it plain
i live among
the ones keep an eye on
their dying most everyday
kid looks past the cleaner
a simple does a simple
couldn't have gotten luckier
the product leakin
just there

to say it right
we sat in rooms
over night
were brooded clean

member that farmer janitor
cow musk low in the hall

paygrades and raisins
yr callin's to
call the cows
sloweyed on
buttercup volts

destined to live
in stints
ah did you reach
the machine
this many ticks gather
yr thoughts and throw
the umbrella of the mind
money to the broke

slick wrench tight in
oh a pen
edge of the field
for branding purposes
burn it down
wit slab wink

runnin in circles
prepares the planting
down to dirt in
yr crazed head

this machine heals
stint stent stat

drowned 2-by-4 arms
weight of the water
one fat baby keeps
most silence slim

patched his clothes
from the inside
she did she did

the statue's of her his shadow is

buddy holly forever
suspensed in iowa air

could and did do
check yr own hair
in the mirror of his hair

carrot jello eyebrow

so what year is it traditional in yr head

sunrise
neon
doctor
migraine
pylon
sunset

five nights supper tudor tar yr collar

perch shirt
smoke jerk
water drama

go around casual
all the day
a lemon fat fog
so personal to you

start stogie-ing and you'll itch to quit it

one charnel two carnal three carnival

try this best
doorhat nail
to ex out
the day away

startled wing for eye

looks like inside's
hiring for
what will it be
and what'll ya have

currently feelin
thru with all that

this is that

didn't dear brother poet pal steve marvel so

doesn't he tonsil sea scroll

ransom
alone
out
walking

carves a one
straight your knife
moves the
sun

inside's
interested in
hip ham
ham hip
just what day it is

sun doin that egg in a pan
dishwater watch bright thru

somethin about smokin
on a crayon in a canyon
of the mind
feels wren cool

if it burns if they burn
george burns
burns day
ignite the riding gloves
cut from goat throats
enter fingers
swallow say
snug as screams
on screens a quarrel of
grump cuts away

wheel spells eternal spools
only the trip's timed by
how much wheels wear

a graveyard for rolling road is road is
wheel does the mother drone

only place we can't live's the circle
bullshit say the birds
only place we can is the square

stretched wheel
bow triangled
the feather trigger
another name for
eye be bucket try

the hole in it
to fence with it
steady leaky faucet clock
a cattail a fern

the harmless gurney yr shadow sometimes is
hickory smock

these spring eaves faster gladder

or time is the time
it takes to kiss
all of the belly
careful to be
spitty enough

the lips slather about
like a kingsea bingo dauber
or a holy water
simple dish
wet cloth therein
touch the stamp
three times be sure
with corners

woodpecker startled plenty some none

out past young
i burn the deck for uncertain reasons

flame is a drunk to his feet like a charm
and sideways in wind

seems whole but several must
same sound as the needled pine
preaches a carved hole
thru it and thru it the train

cartoon germs vowel swarms

cheek fat cave bear grin fish hey hey

tendon scarp
on the loose
hey hey

inside's where
all the stories are

try this one on
washed enough
in the mouth to be
shrunk down some

a struggle to get into

and why does my mouth say try

it was her birthday
he was on a blackout drunk
chased her out the house

her into the buick for once the sags
in the ceilin fabrics nobody is complaining
gravel lives a little

courts the air
compliments of gas slam

him leaping onto the back bumper onto the back
him getting dragged up past the mailbox

it is her birthday again
he stands for
redefining standing
it's okay to say
like an animal bucket
of water tossed on a fire

his mouth in the rearview and she's going
quick his rotten apple mouth raw
gnawed by rabbit wind and pinked
with morning headache light

so when he lifts his shirt next afternoon
innocent as a baby bleach bottle fulla calf gonads
and fortified wine
all the little welty cuts and cuts and scratches

looks like that mouth
of his took out walking
on the moon gut
or new snow
light as burned bills
ghost nose hairs
daddy pastures

no schoolyards to mow

tight and strange
no flags to show
the silent cutting wind
in rust we trust

whatever it takes
to moo eyes
moos eyes
moose eyes
moose mouse eyes yes

muumuus half off
3 more hours
genuine vintage
and countin

i and chickens sittin
twistin desks it's this
lunch bean
another power

the jaw works
like a jerk
like it likes to
like a tractor tire

ever roll thru water
and feel you were
the first to wag
a wagon wheel

patience being

a wheel
width issue

water being a negotiation
recognition
troll con
stubby bridge
swallows from the underside
catch the light catch the light
skim the river
like nervous folks
tuggin at the edges
of wherever whatever fabric ends

worry over half ya know
in just pass one
across this field

askt if he was ever lonely
with all that tractorin
to do and none but him
to do it

kids' legs not long enough yet or ever

uncle monty
spokes his eyes
in smile lines
like a kid drawin eyelashes
on the sun says soft as
a radio personality
with a coughdrop in

i sing all day sing all day
oceanfront property

and the hawks sing
like they're pissin fire
like they're freezin blood
to where you can work with it
and the mice run
like furry sparkplug dejecta
their hearts blue earplugs
in dust bunnies in every corner
a sock and the coldest thing
was that river in spring
and the hottest thing
was the cannin jar coolin

fierce little matchhead burst
the thirsty flame
this chickadee's heart
shortest day of the year

or whiskers on a shrew mole grow
like fuses burn duties quieting

stay burnt cloud says

see i must have me some cold cloud dna

for real sale kite flannel
don't fly just sits laid out
like a cat made
of old mousetraps

that's right that's where
the clothesline strung
occasional and unofficial finch
tobacco honey plug
little thistle eater
cheese dust pouch

                .

yes sun can paint in lines and outly

that's right they took and
verticaled poles on them
old laundry t's and painted the
shootin match yellow scream
and got the kid kickin
fieldgoals rain or shine
snow or sleet bees it
didn't matter which way
the wind blew there was opportunity
for three and three and three
and three

sometimes last year's seeds shake nice within

sound late like this within within three three

whereas ever
later gourds grow
in consternation
conversation
with balloons

in five

months the leaves
the tongues
the ruddy cuds
the friday housepainters
throw their
neatenin rags
down

i see speechlessness
is the coming summer's
blood

and the leaves shall run
bended knees
the angles of
foot on free chair
cranky shoe
got tied

and the leaves dead give
the urine smell

live trees go
every direction
like horse piss on a man's hat
like mechanical wind and teen speed
as the story tends to beat the deed
ah with britches once worn on the moon
he whited out where he went
blizzarded the buzzard

don't be an ingrate just migrate

to watch a tree

is to read a long book
every little twist
and confounded conniption joe
sure to touch the burner
cuza badinage of yesterday
the cousin kiss and more
in secret treat fort x
behind the dump y
where the dozers z
guided by widehead men
erupt clouds
dirty faithful

the leaves
like a bloody nose
farmer blow

like bubbles
trailin the swimmer
slow thought
first thing
in the mornin

shall fall watered fire
or matin birds
or dyin birds

or fireworks
ember pleasurers

snowin gold
snowin golden

snowin goldenly
who is counting
only the heart is
for there is
no higher math
than blood in motion

write you a check
but the bank is far
much farther than you
have ever gone
so you'll just have to see
yrself with yr mind
rollin in it

and the old oak leaves
fall like puppet spiders
in a rain old folks
wavin at you thru the curtains
parted and the men
in the towns
with those canes of wind
scatter things
out of sight out of mind
this is life

this is me
crawling up
to glue such what

back to limb bow
life for life
leave to arrive
how is it may and i am seeing autumnally

the poet eye cidery

arrive to leave

may one
soft as they are
the leaves say va va
puppy ear insides

mighty much
getting used to
ears like weeds
you pick
what runs underneath
is so much deeper
than any lowtime whistlin
thin green stray
seems needs

day may
may day

everything recovering

skinny sky light like the bloody mary
the morning after
what last ice releases

ditch land
and out to the fields
old alcoholics all
rolling over
in sick sweet sheets

and did you know the children dream
they make boats
in bottles
with shavings
off your fingerbones

the sails endless
gauze fuss occlusions

is your father your father's violence

did a child pen a tired old man face
on a mushroom
among mushrooms
log teeth

seemed to be always there
him gone or there
in the doorway there
in the only way to pass thru there
from room to room there

the bear den
under the coyote den
under the badger den

and the quiet bite bite bite
of your endless retelling

how the dogs licked
aunt dirtier
her loneliness or
their tongue wet shine
when the storm cut the power
we saw by the light of the pooch spit upon

and you find yrself
all any would wanna say
they did do
yes it was a sunday
or maybe monday
when i found myself

close rememberin
like yr cuttin
paper cat eyes
and eatin them

faux eucharist
that's a lot of my youth

yeah buddy
fruitflies like promises
made by folks
out no wheels

yesterday
as seen thru

the fake barf
of tomorrow

chunkin spume

one truth and 2 lies

i only eat
peaches while
talkin taxes on my
burner phone

about time
to run
some vinegar
thru that coffee pot

primitive vaccination

guy what lost his wind
got part pig heart
right now

see him sometimes
down tired roads
jumpropin gravel
spittin off his swingin
like shy parade candy
with a temper

while the present moment
makes dispensational fools

of the kitchen clock's
heart dusts sealed
in oils fell
thru the airs
got caught

as angel boot bird
does do
in yr deadwood
scum mulch dreams

flip every little piece
and there she is
that bad stuff
what you don't want
nort need

not so one out walking

of course a curve happens
carvin one i out walkin
is most natural

must leave
a little space
for the dead many
to be enough
firm rising
firm for rising
for our rising

medium hard

is a real good
egg order
and adios way
us unbent
thank you
we agree

suckers for hollyhocks
since birth maybe

if trauma is generational why not beauty

vireo mind
pay no mind
to the rooster

among roosters

whose boiled eye's
sperm and gong

unreliable narrator of light
egg light
simple drool upon the pillowcase light

strange fictions
gathering on the pillow
mastodon cave paintings
drunk by the flood

water is endless mouth
and stories

forgotten fast as said

ocean knows hotter just as sky with fire
smoke being everything
like a crowded room

one gentle knuckle
counter mocktail wise
against the clit
of the eye

rooster yoga
is a good idea
chill dictator chill

those tiny apple basket
paper cups
for fast food ketchups
these bloods from the bodies
of former menacers

and there's a god
weary from the road
long hair strawy
courteous wind
piecing things

pushin
the plunger
down

and push and turn and spin
seal the napoleon

squirtgun
fulla iodine and rubbin alcohol
in yonder bird

now you now you

hey i'd be pissed too
if i had wings
and was nothin
but a ground scuffler

say yr great uncle was a steel trap

and you only look to see
the shit you can fuck up

ears niagara with rose blood

i know it now
the heart is a curtain
weeping

everything said gets
writ with an eraser

the consequential nothing cozying

there's an odd scrounge effect

otter dart otter dart if you will

stuck on the ruddy rudder

whoopee cushion face
of this next one over

have you heard some guys

fall in a chair
i wouldn't lie to ya
sound like gettin a flat tire
from a chicken bone
to me

face dawn shout
blood in the fridge
tabasco catsup poopoo

gracenotes ya can't hardly sell
dust bath back of the shelf

expectorate a draintrap
up thru still mauve air

mama plumb the light
papa plumb blue
sky crease light

without a hitch how could i
have pulled my
own self thru

pulled it off with style as floydy says

and new night was steel pony

and i with only
lesser train qualities

mornin comes
snark tart told you so

heavy catcher
squattin over
the bidet
exhibition game hotel

every bird
every tree strange
acting like to text a tea
a sweet tea

cheers u fool rooster
for the disjointure
so the light
like water
mine and that that's called forth waiting
has a way

one to three gentle mornin coughs help

as for alcohol
there are alleyways
in the mind
out back of which
coffeecans and sand and cig butts
out back of which
old mop water

weighty water
little floor lotta goin

and these alleyways
around drink number fun numb
fuse to the good streets
chicken neck weasel

owl got the head
weasel got the blood
now yr a racketball ball racket
no a badminton racket
no the birdie and the bird
now nothin but what the sleepin wind says
when whipt

how about the cat
with what teeth did for ears
bellyful of foot and floor
licking the chicken wing sauce
from the filter end of the dead smoke

how about eating the robin's tongue
in a flash and for once
feelin satisfied
in no hurry

how about a rubber chicken
unburied by oceans
of time

for a minute is

revolving
up from under

the great churn
of the dozer
strain
and its dirty paw
and its dirtier wave

ah but how do you spell
fun with the well
no the will
of an abandoned mine

i was the cousin

and the rain coming
no the snow well
ah both at once

and the raccoon
morseling any one
to toy cig many

as when the laugher cries
mouth full of mucus
stretches the spit
like play fangs

is it just me
done with the counting
loving to linger

where road bends

road's generous

has a way
of loving not getting
us there

lonely lovely road
peace rest in gonesville

only accidents
make marks
is not true

but it pleases the heart
to break that way and why

loving lies
about having it
both ways and how
gone i am no-one
known
and most
myself

home i must relearn
how not to be
allergic to my own hair

yes the road scours
everything

but behind the ears

no i can't say how it was
nor how it went
but if you'd like to know
that's right draw yr nose
up close here closer
behind my ear
and breathe careful
like you might try
first day yr senses return

all of them and just one
overgrown rose and roses
eat yardlamps of old
whose glassed birdhouse vibes
everybody is talkin overstrung in
webs and eggs and eggs and webs
riverrock and old dog eye and
dim and bright and written
all over as old skating ice might

fuzzy nuzzlings might
spidery milkings might

the wind machine motion makes
when added to real wind
means storms are only
fetching accelerations away
and half as real or not anyway

how is going good gaining is it

perhaps going is wasting
yrself flyin offa yrself

you the storm behind
you the teeth in rollin blackout
you the camp under the househouse
you geology under that under that
you somethin big mushed to somethin bigger
you the patient face in for camel licking

i have an idea what clean zoo eyes can see

chance and choice hard to tease

ya try and see a chance and choice it

when wind and minutes go wide

in the going peaceness

i look back on my life and see
always seemed to feel
i had a big past

that livin aware in fear
from young among muffled noisy
felt like i was inside
somethin big i couldn't
unhear couldn't unsee

let's call it a soup pot

even when my days and ligaments
were soft as paper dominoes
even when no topple exactatory outlasted seven

i see i seemed to walk the edges
and around and around
what had already happened
when so little had

tho i saw myself warholed
in the sweat slugs
static then sliding
slow then fast
down the necks
of the women canning beans
later summer days
dusk never ends

i see i felt myself solitary
my skin interrupting my bones
from their very own stone cold journeying

you never shd shoot at the buck to the neck
in the cranberries

yes first grow we as grass then as trees

i see i was a little old man
i had my constipation to tend to
i had my knees would slip out of place
haywire as somebody frustrated

with an alarm clock in a precoder
covered in peacocks and the bends

still here i am going
going on
doing better than enduring

at last perched at least
on the edge of the pot
as tho on a cold bleacher
at the last homegame of the year
tossing little moons
and ufo saucers
of onion and potato in

as gramsy said
while i swept her tiny kitchen floor
when she was happiest there
at pheasant lane
looking up from the paper
nothing but milk left in the cereal dish
she'd made a second face
by eating all the cereal away
oh why don't you just step on it

what's moist must move this we know

kid's first car and the wipers
are a total loss
so stands while she drives
and by the elephant trunk
of one coat sleeve

flung out the window
beats at front glass

on her way to the gas
station job the stories
behind the tattoos
begin with plastic gin

guy talks like he has
ass rashes and worse
lips like unfried calamari
and eyes like walnut rot

eyes like old farmer knuckles
seem to rub ya
as you restock
the nyquil blue
as smurf blood

i know hummingbirds

like vaccinations swim ripped pieces

of extension cord wind

greater rivers of wind

sound
like this
is it is it is it

i know the in between's

where yearning goes
to stir and brew

and stir and brew
means stew in heartish

and i know some of us are tuned to yearning
can't help it
it's a little of both i am sure
who we are who were we were made to be

and i know the world can see
this in us

amiably muddy inner rabbit summer salts

can see our eyes
spiritual dust dumps
freighted with all the places

a little gone here

like a juggler
given to glass doorknobs

somehow seems
they are all always in the air

behind her
native purple clouds
move and don't move
could only mean whales

whose song rooms
aspen the ocean

hummingbirds
historical jazzes
corks in rapids

cork jazz tight

hummingbirds watch
us through dust
lag windows
our belly
buttons in
their crayfish eyes

as if they could make a lie
of glass
can and do
and in thru where we were
taken from mother life support

and then to fashion
beautiful clothes inside
our own skin lime pudding
gowns and checked tapioca trousers

this is the story of how
we came to become
blood on the inside
little trails of tailor's thumb-pricks
dribble on seep

ah it's rainin
artesianally

and when will you love yourself
wholly which is to say
forget yourself entirely

today is the day

coming is going is coming is going

in our eyebrows
the road dust suspended
flesh ash on the foreheads
of the believing
and them that lean
into the bedroom wall
of their own burned down house know

gravel simply the hardest dust

reach down
and try my finger

the one meant to mean the way
to this gravel face

one of 8 sides on this piece alone

janus in a mirrored hall

and bring back up

dust from road
and quarry both

dust soft as
the kindest person
you can think of
putting on clothes

edge of a bed
gives a little

in a room
whose sunshine
in through sheer drapes

quiets the dust

eager to instigate
tender considerations
of all those worlds

and worldly countings

who here hears this dust panting
raise yr hand fist

alarm clocks can't
or can they

fell in with
the green beans
at the canning factory

ticking fists

now we
wield an opener
yield an opening
just to know
it's early still

so does everything get easier over time
or does everything grow harder
like old people toenails
and is this to do with how hope works

and is hope a blindness
couple degrees shy
of simmering in
our own relative
comfort sauce

or is hope
what it is
to trade yr
teeth for eyes

must grin out to see

i must learn the courage
not to know

hope this leather suppler

think of ant

the ant
each one stone
up and over
up and over

hat found itself its calling
as they say when flipped
for berries

it's not a call to feel
it just is
it's just what is

the canopy
guess what
that's what
that's right

keeps night
like nostalgia

this air here
the air here
air here

colder than i am
pickin coffee grounds
from my teeth

no tellin what all chickens will eat
one egg and i am wired
dead in a pond

playin a mouthharp
wadded up old underwear
no pizzaboxes
no underwear

please explain energy drink to grandpa

please behave like your silverware
is ordered and shining
no haste crumbs
no hairs fallen like wind thru the upside
down u pail handle
of hope

and jam jars
and bygone mayo
and busted tires that don't look busted

talk like old people eat
seen some things
when you jump on 'em

i know only one song

but when i change
my clothes
switch chairs
and outlast sunday
you'll go
for it

in through

the still and silent oaks

where quiet is

oak skin
eyes on
distills the trouble
dried on the rocks

scattering

effortless as swinging
down on a shorter nail

just beyond
these dips those
seasonal ponds

rung around
with ferns gone greener
when bear piss sun
middles all

i feel i am the heartburn
in sun throat
directorly

and there's the essential
mercies of trees
their shade a cave of the mind

what sun arrives upon

work or none done

sifty sifty sifty

feels like staging
foraging

lost in the sheets on the line
eyes shut and counting

well it was supposed to
be ten but between you
and me i only made nine

who knew ghosts sweat chill
i didn't until i write it

for sunlight
chairs are plentiful

no thanks been sitting all day

sucha drama hound this light

lifts you up by the ear

see where light is eye is

i didn't even know i was curious

the skin on my skull floating that way

crisis free i feel eerie i feel cozy
long and short is
i am alive all the way
when peace ends

deerfly

many
many
many
just a few given
to exceptional
hustle

physicality

up lift boot

it's hard to stop and count and think

cheerleader megaphone
shouted backwards
through
ear fur of that

lazy badger
larkin
in tha culvert

baby head in
the lion swell

them flies they
invert
duncecaps

them flies they
starchy
insomniac
nightcaps

them flies they
cone on in
down pointy
pointy

tips creaming

like to write yr name
on urinal cakes

truckstop somewhere out there
you know the feeling
it's not healthy
this breathless pissin

soap's a piece
eroding in
yellowing grey

grin

no use running
everything you do

yr very alive aliveness

ties you in
draws them in

eye wild back
like fire on a coat
like poisoned milkweed
useless rearin reachin
sprayin

no chemical gonna
skull 'em back to the scullery

to them
you are a storm
on tv

to them you are sooner oklahoma

crimson aquifer on legs

the last and only answer
to the question of eggs

go on
no
go on
no
go on

good luck's a freezer

door ajar forgotten
until the morning

a mush leak
happened waits
here on the floor

that chair works good
for drying your socks
room temperature fever didn't i unsay

a luck a joke
the wrong fuck
takes personally

when he stands up
mountain in the mirror
the patrons
eat the music

around the first corner
on the run

you know where we are now

sweatin and swearin
school forest land aft
something near a mile

a little dip
a little level

some beaver some bear

some beaver cleaning out and
a creek that runs when the county guys say

and a composting body stench

now which plant is that
always gets ma

to fearing the sow with cubs

or unsquare young gun one
dangerously low
on family

used to be just them
the one couple that whole stretch
young back then
she works the feedstore still
downy arms and eyes clear as winter breath

eager generosity
almost elfish curiosity

tho as she's aged and
slamming an only slightly sturdy
baby carriage then two
over the gravels has
developed an admittedly reasonable
annoyance with our clownish
pouncing entire bookshelf

falling on the pinky toe
barking dogs

and he's a good guy
mellow happy guy
keep an eye out guy
factory guy
appreciates its edges

whistles a little when he speaks
is mostly deaf

once recalled
how much he loved his life now
to read at night just
think of it reading at night he says
me doing that

growing up he says
farming like that
only time we ever
read was when we was in the can

and there was an understanding
in a family that size
such things were timed

glass and sand complicitly slipping
until the shins they are blinding

are you done in there hey

the books going inchy
as rained on newspaper
to a flame

what books
it was implement mags
and one mauled readers digest
looked like it survived
falling in
at least a few times

more than twice
and it did

and you must never forget it
this field planted for hunters
come up now and again
from the townish cities
and burbs cold with guns
with weedeater fourwheeler
snowmobile sidebyside
make some noise

was once one tractor only
and horses times before that
and this william of ours was set upon
by deerfly right here
no right here

can you feel it still
raspberries
pick their teeth with their own thorns

and beehived down

but he had the corn to cultivate
and it wasn't something
had another time written on it
so steady as she goes

and was this william set upon
waving his hat
like to catch a butterfly
high on life

bull lonely
he wasn't what he lookt like
a glue ass cowboy dandy
hat doffed
and donned and doffed
and donned

welts gave way to inflamements

come home like he forgot
every line
in the play of the self dolt
got launched at
by rotten cherry tomato

much of his inner self
on religious display

did they doctor it
did he ever

tries for years
linymints

the doctor sayin it's gone over
to hives it's in you now

at night waking like with a bat feather
playing at museum dusting
up his strong sunwork nose

felt a fly backfloat like a frog
through the little tame sweet
sway thames veins

and his wife's great uncle
shook hands
with lincoln
at gettysburg

this i know and now you do too

and i inherited many of his ballcaps
i can show you some
sometime maybe
you can look
you can't touch

and this fella william
lived to be 95 and change

last time i seen him
he said boys it's

curtains for me
it's curtains

and he was a little waxy
and i told him
my hand on the bone
his shoulder'd become
fast the truth
was i loved him
and prayed for him
just as natural as i walked
around on a good day
no gut ache
no hangover you know of anyway

and his great big chair
got bigger
him in it shrinking
by the take
the taking cancer
but you gotta take

them all saying you got to try and take something to eat

and i called him
william tho he was always
bill because dying
feels formal

and the longer the name the longer the stay
and the time we have is the great unknown

and some are travelers
and some are mud suckers
and i've never known a dog
to pass up a puddle

as for me
when i pass one
i stoop in
and wave
at the above

for angels
use puddles
for messages

such as tick tick tick
or is it tsk tsk

that's me imitating
wheels in bombs
a heart's not that round

and he smiled at me somethin like a gate
to a field opening

and i smiled at him
somethin like coyote full on raccoon full on corn

and that was the last time i seen him
with these my temporary eyes

the pigeons back around now

beating off on the sky
like a guy walking around
town with a detached sole

and his conservative
daughter and her
liberal neighbor
a most curious pair
sit in lawnchairs
from the 1980s
just outside the yawning
mouth of the garage
staring at the pines
out across the road
their dusky dark greenness inhaling all

their eyes raisin soft
as folks will do when
watching nowhere
only to hear one another
confidinger

and it's a pretty busy road
why i can't tell you really
a word they say
folks say when they go inside
they wash their hands
with kitchen sink water
and dry their hands
on each other's shirts

if shadows in windows

if you believe shadows in windows
translate that way

funny how bendy night can feel
what we can say then
that was dead impossible
in the sun grope day

and when he laught
he embarked upon laughter
he got er goin
with a little ether

he went tee hee
tee hee tee hee

as fer them damned flies
why bring yr hand
in a blind
neck back wipe

why see if you can make 'em history

why some smear and tumble
soon beat to nothing
by truck wheels

why some stun a second
entering
air again
a touch of the inside
come out

chickens chase spat seeds
but it's rinds they love

as fer them damned flies
i too love to imagine
crookeder flights

the retold story
of a near miss
tends to render a person
a little more gentle

long as almost is
a modesty cap
aired out on the nail
always feels a little greased
by the latest effort

doff and swing
doff and swing
something like the kid
can't get the hang
of badminton

something about the birdie
mainly air
thwarts those
stuck on gravity

getting used to varying rates
of falling seems like a fair way
to talk about handling

what life leads you through

it's only getting haunted
dandelion fluff
painted on the armpits
helps

it's the thing doesn't quite fall
the ghost ya wanna beat

something like a puddle
writing down the barn
struck by lightning

apt way enough to say a life

i am not sure you saw it then
so here you are here you go
stories are ecologies
the more you tell the one
the less the guardian picks up

too busy throwing tarps
in fires
to see the likes
of plastic jump

sorta the hens-teeth comes with refroze ice

soon enough see
far as the eye can
these stuntmen

close enough to be you
they got the right leg heft alright
bent double
from a bad lunch
or was it
a hard contact lens

what good's a caddy in the woods

does every song have to remind ya of another song

days abrade days

they are more than a little adhesive

and the deerfly sit ya
two little handsaws
big on a small face
commence to the
back and forth
baccalaureate fort
sore back cuza the ford

and they easel bite yr finger neck skin

and they scuff an x cut in yr skin

and i sing of the blood brother pacts
schwinns' kickstands kicked and leaning
like shy deer toward the flies sawing
while just there
in the dirty shadow of the abandoned shack

palm to palm to palm to palm sticky we
mingle vermillion iron soft
drifting into one another
like the songs of coyotes
like winter snakeballs
like swallows smokin
a little dragonfly reefer

and they scuff an x cut in yr skin
in every western movie this is how it's done
and suck and spit while the face of the hiss nipped
sweats something like oil nickels

and we understand time has gone by
when her hair looks like the side of the road in winter
and there's air there
where the arm or leg was

now that yr flowin goin outta yrself
now they lower the mop called the mouth

is that an eyeholeless skull head
no that's a blue ribbon puffball mushroom
big like they grow 'em
anywhere the lonely pony broods

sorta like to lower yr skull
a piglet of risen dough
into the cistern
hot with water from sulfur springs

and they mop what's fresh from you

and they do it all
quick as fish or bird

how did the fella stay on the bucker that long
how do these she-flies
us bucking hold
and business us like that

the will to say
i am paper dolls the arms
gone right into hands
and back up again
is soft iron

that feeling you
are jumping
on yrself
in the noonday sun
is soft iron

and we must have what's next

their flying to the underside
of low leaves
and other convenient green junks

must have what's next

go on go on go on go on

party's nothin
but pushovers

hard to say
how they feel
chins nodding
like you are reading
the words they love flowering
from stem and stamen
of each of their
eyebrow hairs

go on go on go on go on

among the man flies
their eyes close
to touching
what do they do
so very little
most important
get eaten by
dragonfly
and swallow
good boy
good egg
you smudged out
your life almost out
tryin to

you gave up
yr space nice
about the length
of the fox's tooth
about the length
of the ice milk mirage

these little pieces
of rice these little
children gather
from the cathedral
steps and know
the holding in
the human mouth
takes about a day
of please and thankyou
to cook a piece of
rice in the human way
faster if you jerks
your stones in your snowballs
come runnin

and why do mouths go sideways
like chairs too much sat in
in a jeer

and why do gal deerfly
have eyes so far
apart me
i am often
busy seeing
everything at once
while the magnet
part of my mind
brings a gentle
suck upon one thing

would be no affection without affect otherwise

i need not pose a question
when i am floods of 'em

questing
gal fly
gold eye

old but on
computer screens kicked
by kids trying to be
someone seen
on computer screens

something metal
decaying prettily

fresh water standing
nasty salute
to algae bloom

gold for eyes
and eyes for gold
it's a shame how much
we refresh our accounts

one way to
divvy folks into buckets
those that do
and them that don't
or those that won't
some who can't
without a bus

to the library
you have 30 minutes
starting now

folks who forget they
have money waiting
in paychump or venmoo
i will never ever understand

we wriggled up from different ponds

see they mop up the bloodmeal
like a dry guy in a western
where water seeps from rock

and they egg up the water edges
and the undersides of what have you

what's next is
time might
see what's on
the stove in
the teevee

what's next is
a larval go
at zooplankton and the like

what's next is
grubbin around
below the freeze line

i see a cursive
like oldtime trick pilots
thru winter lard
an automatics truing certain dormancies
see the gentlest tether is the wink

and did you leave the stove on
did you lock that up right
and do you really sign yr name
like a plastic bag making
sexual sounds
on a fence

and where are your keys
and why are they
in the door again
like a painting of
a hummingbird
head-deep in a trumpet vine flower
like an oldtime photographer
head flung under the dark cloth
stay still stay still stay still

and where in the world
did you learn
to eat yr teeth
walk like you wipe
the mouth of
dead folks
with every fallfoot

longer i know myself

the more i see myself
as from long ago

and love is saying i am nowhere near where you are

or here is a yarn green string
it is long and plenty strong

so let us let the ants of our affectionate goodness
tightrope across
tickle is talking fairly way
the bridge knotty
with lovers locks
right here the guy got
his head chopped
off we heard the sound
and run up and there was the guy
one place and his ideas
over there and nothin
but yellow and red in between

in the river one morning
there with the rocks
and fish like thoughts bending
something new

a stopsign

and did i run
to tell bob
and did i pedal
to tell florence

bob down through the poison ivy
and wild asparagus

bob in his river shoes
canvas with toes
cut out and dangling

bob draggin the sign
like a body
or the shovel edge
spills a groove
you take and
scatter the seed
in there

and there was a number
he had to call and
it would take some time
to find in the book

red sign paintin
the grasses
with the river
right now

Abraham Smith was raised around Ladysmith, Wisconsin, and lives in Ogden, Utah, where he is associate professor of English and co-director of Creative Writing at Weber State University. His recent poetry collections include *Insomniac Sentinel* (Baobab Press, 2023) and *Dear Weirdo* (Propeller Books, 2022). Away from his desk, Smith improvises poems inside songs with the Snarlin' Yarns: thesnarlinyarnsut.bandcamp.com.

This project was made possible, in part, by generous support from the Osage Arts Community.

Osage Arts Community provides temporary time, space and support for the creation of new artistic works in a retreat format, serving creative people of all kinds — visual artists, composers, poets, fiction and nonfiction writers. Located on a 152-acre farm in an isolated rural mountainside setting in Central Missouri and bordered by ¾ of a mile of the Gasconade River, OAC provides residencies to those working alone, as well as welcoming collaborative teams, offering living space and workspace in a country environment to emerging and mid-career artists. For more information, visit us at www.osageac.org

Osage Arts Community